THIS JOURNAL BELONGS TO

Gabriella Guerrero ♡

SHINE BRIGHT

PRODUCTIVITY JOURNAL

CHRONICLE BOOKS
SAN FRANCISCO